TRUMPET

HAL•LEONARD
BIG BAND
PLAY-ALONG
VOLUME 4

Jazz Classics

ISBN 978-1-4234-4986-7

HAL•LEONARD®
CORPORATION
7777 W. BLUEMOUND RD. P.O. BOX 13819 MILWAUKEE, WI 53213

Visit Hal Leonard Online at
www.halleonard.com

HAL·LEONARD
BIG BAND
PLAY-ALONG
VOLUME 4

Jazz Classics

BAGS' GROOVE

By MILT JACKSON
Arranged by MARK TAYLOR

TRUMPET

TRUMPET

BLUE 'N BOOGIE

Trumpet

By JOHN "DIZZY" GILLESPIE and FRANK PAPARELLI
Arranged by MARK TAYLOR

TRUMPET

BLUE TRAIN
(BLUE TRANE)

TRUMPET

By JOHN COLTRANE
Arranged by MARK TAYLOR

DOXY

By SONNY ROLLINS
Arranged by MARK TAYLOR

Trumpet

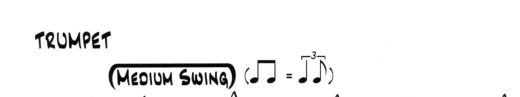

TRUMPET

FOUR

By MILES DAVIS
Arranged by MARK TAYLOR

Trumpet

TRUMPET

MOTEN SWING

Trumpet

By BUSTER MOTEN and BENNIE MOTEN
Arranged by SAMMY NESTICO

TRUMPET

OLEO

By SONNY ROLLINS
Arranged by MARK TAYLOR

TRUMPET

TRUMPET

SONG FOR MY FATHER

TRUMPET

Words and Music by HORACE SILVER
Arranged by MARK TAYLOR

TRUMPET

STOLEN MOMENTS

Words and Music by OLIVER NELSON
Arranged by MARK TAYLOR

Trumpet

TRUMPET

STRAIGHT NO CHASER

Trumpet

By THELONIOUS MONK
Arranged by MARK TAYLOR

TRUMPET

THE BIG BAND PLAY-ALONG SERIES

These revolutionary play-along packs are great products for those who want a big band sound to back up their instrument, without the pressure of playing solo. They're perfect for current players and for those former players who want to get back in the swing!

Each volume includes:

- Easy-to-read, authentic big band arrangements
- Professional recordings on CD of all the big band instruments, including the lead part
- Editions for alto sax, tenor sax, trumpet, trombone, guitar, piano, bass, and drums

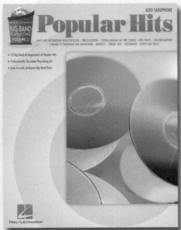

1. SWING FAVORITES

April in Paris • I've Got You Under My Skin • In the Mood • It Don't Mean a Thing (If It Ain't Got That Swing) • Route 66 • Speak Low • Stompin' at the Savoy • Tangerine • This Can't Be Love • Until I Met You (Corner Pocket).

07011313 Alto Sax $14.95
07011314 Tenor Sax $14.95
07011315 Trumpet $14.95
07011316 Trombone $14.95
07011317 Guitar $14.95
07011318 Piano $14.95
07011319 Bass $14.95
07011320 Drums $14.95

2. POPULAR HITS

Ain't No Mountain High Enough • Brick House • Copacabana (At the Copa) • Evil Ways • I Heard It Through the Grapevine • On Broadway • Respect • Street Life • Yesterday • Zoot Suit Riot.

07011321 Alto Sax $14.95
07011322 Tenor Sax $14.95
07011323 Trumpet $14.95
07011324 Trombone $14.95
07011325 Guitar $14.95
07011326 Piano $14.95
07011327 Bass $14.95
07011328 Drums $14.95

3. DUKE ELLINGTON

Caravan • Chelsea Bridge • Cotton Tail • I'm Beginning to See the Light • I'm Just a Lucky So and So • In a Mellow Tone • In a Sentimental Mood • Mood Indigo • Satin Doll • Take the "A" Train.

00843086 Alto Sax $14.95
00843087 Tenor Sax $14.95
00843088 Trumpet $14.95
00843089 Trombone $14.95
00843090 Guitar $14.95
00843091 Piano $14.95
00843092 Bass $14.95
00843093 Drums $14.95

4. JAZZ CLASSICS

Bags' Groove • Blue 'N Boogie • Blue Train (Blue Trane) • Doxy • Four • Moten Swing • Oleo • Song for My Father • Stolen Moments • Straight No Chaser.

00843094 Alto Sax $14.95
00843095 Tenor Sax $14.95
00843096 Trumpet $14.95
00843097 Trombone $14.95
00843098 Guitar $14.95
00843099 Piano $14.95
00843100 Bass $14.95
00843101 Drums $14.95

HAL•LEONARD® CORPORATION

7777 W. BLUEMOUND RD. P.O. BOX 13819 MILWAUKEE, WI 53213

Prices, contents and availability subject to change without notice.